Unfathoming

Also by Andrea Cohen

Furs Not Mine
Kentucky Derby
Long Division
The Cartographer's Vacation

Unfathoming

Andrea Cohen

Four Way Books
Tribeca

Please direct all inquiries to:
Editorial Office
Four Way Books
POB 535, Village Station
New York, NY 10014
www.fourwaybooks.com

Library of Congress Cataloging-in-Publication Data

Names: Cohen, Andrea, 1961- author.
Title: Unfathoming / Andrea Cohen.
Description: New York : Four Way Books, [2017]
Identifiers: LCCN 2016034896 | ISBN 9781935536840 (softcover : acid-free paper)
Classification: LCC PS3603.O3415 A6 2017 | DDC 811/.6--dc23
LC record available at https://lccn.loc.gov/2016034896

This book is manufactured in the United States of America and printed on acid-free paper.

Four Way Books is a not-for-profit literary press. We are grateful for the assistance
we receive from individual donors, public arts agencies, and private foundations.

This publication is made possible with public funds from the National Endowment for the Arts

and from the New York State Council on the Arts, a state agency.

We are a proud member of the Community of Literary Magazines and Presses.

Distributed by University Press of New England
One Court Street, Lebanon, NH 03766

for Naomi Wallace

CONTENTS

THREE

FOUR

I'm bored to death, I can't go out
because of the bad weather.
I wish I were two little dogs
so I could play together.

—Godfried Bomans

ONE

String Theory

It's not that
complicated: string

exists. It bundles
beets or quartets

together. Why
should this

be controversial?
Because strings

fray, they tangle.
Because, without

thinking, I'm twisting
my one string into

a noose-shaped heart.

Door-to-Door

Foot in the door or door
in the face. I learned early

on (too late) the sales techniques
employed by door-to-door

salesmen. Instead, I stood
by the window, where you

could see me. I sharpened
my knives and showed how

easily they could slice through
me. I saw your lips moving,

as if commanding a dagger
remotely. I forgot what I

was selling. You were selling
doors beyond my price range:

bullet-proof doors, doors
that opened solely for the past.

Why did I think I was selling
knives? I was selling tears,

and a thousand salesmen
had knocked before me.

Vocation

I've always been a manager
of darkness, for as long

as I can recall. Yes, I'm
self-taught. I started by

embarking, parking candles
and lamps and nursery rhymes

with moonlight roadside. I
stepped away from the road.

Pitfalls? The whip and the chair:
they're instruments the dark

yawns at. You learn that
early on. Every darkness

is different: you feel your way
in, then it tames you.

Poison Hotline

It's got one operator
and two numbers, one

harried taker of incoming
whose job it is to listen

and sound unalarmed, to
first do no harm by recalling

which number a caller
at the end of her tether

has called. One number
offers antidotes for poisons

taken mistakenly. The other
instructs how to bake

a Bundt cake with hemlock.
Keeping it straight is a lot

to ask of one insomniac, who
on quiet nights dials one

number from the other, taking
turns as a certain injured

party, practicing for when
he gets back to the dark

still house and talks
himself through it.

Bedside

Mid-drought, more sun.
When did the tumbler

of water, bedside, fill
with dust? When did you

discover you were a river-
bed no river would touch?

Puzzle

You can make
a puzzle from anything:

just cut stuff up—
an hour, an echocardiogram.

Rearrange the pieces.
Pour yourself

a rainy afternoon,
a blouse by the sea.

Sit at a table
by a picture window.

Don't worry
that the pieces

of the table or
the window or

your own crooked
smile don't quite

fit. It's a puzzle.
Make piles of blue,

of black, of rain.
Let the pieces

sift together: it
only looks like ruin.

Outage

I need a flashlight to find
the flashlight, but make

do without, feeling my
way down the basement

stairs, brailing my hands
along the packed shelves where we

keep flashlights, canned peas, the crank
radio—what's good in an emergency. I

am the emergency vehicle, carrying
the flashlight upstairs. We is

a pronoun I'm told to give up—
like red meat or too much bourbon. It's

dark out and in. The taxi is small
and white, like a hospital

far off. You're leaving me
in the dark, for a mountain

retreat. You seem like a mountain
retreating. I seem like a person—

stiff upper lip—waving goodbye
to a mountain. It's a tantric

retreat, you confess. You suspect
it will be dark where you're going—

a dark different from this one, in which
I give you the flashlight and a weak

thumbs-up and watch you in night
fog fade: lightship pulling anchor.

What I Did on Winter Vacation

I invented a wheel.
It wheeled itself away.

I invented another, with
much fanfare and much

the same outcome.
I'd invent mass

production, but I couldn't
bear their mass migration.

First Things First

I loved my first
love, though I didn't

call her that then.
Then the boat we

were tipped over, and over
and over to the rescue

team she pleaded:
me first. First things

hurt, then we burn
for second, for third yearnings.

Anyone into Anything

after James Richardson

In Ovid, desire can change
anyone into anything. Last

I looked, we weren't
in Ovid, and the problem

was too much desire.
You're still the thick-

headed jug of beauty.
I'm the dustbowl a few

orioles flirt their wings
in, then fly off.

Abandoned House

Finally, a place
I felt at home—
a stone's throw
from your home,
and so much I
could throw:
abandoned knives,
banjo unstrung,
the bland piano.
Abandoned houses
are full of what
was, and up
in the attic,
a few spent bees
in the windowsill
still pulse their last
urgency—having given
up on flowers.

Still Life

We say
that: *still*

life, the way
we say *stay*

to the dog
already gone.

Branch Water

It's what you mix
with bourbon, which is

what gets blended with
ups and downs and those

still evenings when you
wait for the stillness

to get stirred up.
Branch water doesn't

come from a tree,
but from a branch

of the river. It's
a river you go down

once, with or without
a paddle, companion,

or compass, with
or without water.

The Fall of Lawless Bodies

They fall up—
a blizzard
in reverse.
You can't talk
them down.
Lawless bodies,
in their anti-gravity
boots and mittens,
won't listen. But
it only seems
they're smitten
with the stratosphere's
glistening. Really,
it takes all
their lawlessness
not to fall back-
wards: to lose
you twice
might break them.

Ladder

She'd asked everyone
else, so why not ask

the man with the ladder:
Where is origami

for beginners?
Follow me, he says.

She can't even tell
that his ladder's

made of paper
folded over and over

by his paper hands,
which, assisted by

his ladder, will hang
a paper blossom.

She doesn't even
know her own heart,

gathered and pleated,
is an artifact that yet

can turn into a bird.

TWO

Task Lighting

The miner's lamp brightens
dark truths, what we already

knew: the working man never
has enough hands or eyes.

The candle in the garment
district flickers, then flames out

the third-floor window on the skirts
of a girl from Lawrence, Mass.

Actual wattage may vary,
depending on flames and

incandescence, on the trajectory
of men descending and women

falling. There's a task for every
light. It's the right sun rising

and settling on the dimness
of tenements we've yet to invent.

Nights With

Nights with carcasses teach you to count
your lucky stars, they teach you who

you are and aren't: lucky you
are not the calf your half-hour

must debone, nor the night
manager who delights in inviting

a knife to tease the new girl's shirt.
You're not the night or the carcass,

but the man who sees
through them, into the next room,

which is a pasture where the night
manager in a corner stands and writes

I'm sorry in the damp air until
he means it and the night

vanishes and the carcasses
come back to life and nurse the flesh

wounds of the new girl and her
unblemished flesh too. They tell

her: *it could have been worse,* and
even when night comes, it isn't.

Or Pinocchio (When Inside the Whale)
after Justice Stephen Breyer

So much floats—wash tubs, cakes
     of soap, corks, ice, the life
          jacket empty or full, not to mention

          fishing nets, the door unhinged, the trunk
     of a tree that was—but to say
that what floats is a vessel would be a mistake.

Density's the key here, and anecdotally,
     one shoe floats more readily than two,
          as do oil, torpedoed fish, and tin

          cans glinting. But none of these possess
     rudder or sextant, sail, engine, slave
or captain's quarters, nor ship's log,

nor the fear of running aground—all
     aspects typical of vessels. Even
          Saturn, lighter than water, is no vessel,

          or Pinocchio (when inside the whale).
     Outside the whale, Pinocchio paddling madly
with Gepetto toward shore, having endured

hunger, torture, prison, betrayal, not to mention
     waking as a donkey, praying to be made
          a real boy, is of course a vessel.

Tornado

Woman comforting an injured
dog, the caption the morning

after the tornado says, but
if you click for the bigger

picture, the text changes to
woman comforting an injured

and dying dog. It's the same
image, enlarged and without

hope, unless you count
the act of kneeling beside

the dying, unless you keep
your eye trained on the woman's

hand gentling the dog's
breakage, unless you believe

there's something like a soul
capable in high winds of

sheltering, of re-emerging.

Flow Chart

You don't want to see your face
on page 1 connected to other sweating mugs

by yellow arrows and dollar figures
depicted as sacks of gold and darkened

profiles denoting undercover agents.
In a sting operation, they set you

up, they dangle the carrot of a tricked-
out mirror. You do what you shouldn't.

Unless money changes hands, it isn't
a story, my first boss, Alberto, said.

He'd come from Brazil, with rain
on his hands. Money changed them.

I change dollars into pennies to feel
their heft, then change them back.

I'm not worth the paper I'm lifted from.
I steer clear of flow charts because I'm

prone to seasickness. I only want my face
connected to yours in the Hideaway Lounge

by a vague gaze no undercover man can
expose, by a promise unspoken/unbroken.

Where the Sugar Dollars

Where the sugar dollars
have not yet reached is

not far: look no farther
than the cane fields,

where a boy wields
a machete half his size.

What is the size of
injustice? Can it be

sliced in half, then that
half slashed? Where does

all that sugar go? Why
do we call it sweet?

Doing the Loop

The rules are made in factories.
The rules are made to be broken.

Broken people see themselves in broken things.
Whole towns of broken people work somehow.

Somehow is not a place.
Yet, you get there and wonder: how?

How, repeated, is a kind of howl.
In wilds and towns, how answers how.

How do you begin or end?
There are no rules: begin again.

Q & A
after Zaqtan

You may ask eleven questions.
Demanding one answer would be foolish, if not unjust.

Justice stood before the shaving mirror.
Orphaned, he was, with no one to show him how to hold the razor.

The razor had been smuggled into a birthday cake.
Cakes had been outlawed, and births, and days.

The days resembled each other.
In the line-up, they all seemed guilty.

Guilty or innocent? the justice was asked.
How could a river let eleven brothers drown one sister?

State of the Nation

Our nation is stockpiling helium.
Our nation consists of Consuelo, Joey, and me.

Me is no way to begin anything.
To be polite, one waits at the end.

Ends are hard.
Think bread heel, think keel sailing off.

Off is how you feel.
An on switch can't change that.

That balloon drifting is our national anthem.
We salute by drifting too.

Easter on the Rio Grande
after Lorca

That sailor whose throat was just cut
has grown another throat, which grows

another cut. It's an old saw: the blade
that goes around comes around, which

is why the sailor throws his voice
into the sea, why I hold a space

in my glacial lungs for him,
why I keep swimming.

Porch Swing, Summer in a Glass

Porch swing, summer in a glass.
Drinks get named for thirsts we discuss.

Discussions skirt deeper thirsts.
Such thirsts burn, turn sand to mirages.

A mirage is a drink the mind mixes.
In a glass marked no it pours out yes.

Yes, the sign says, this door is an entrance.
At the portal, fields flower without end.

End of the road, grim terminus.
We're thirsty, we get force-fed.

In Response To

I called in sick.
This made me feel ill.

I sipped crushed ice.
The ice came from an ice sculpture.

In the shape of my mother.
She sculpted it before she left.

The resemblance is uncanny.
Maybe everything that melts resembles itself.

I'm feeling a little better.
Well enough to look myself in the mirror.

To start carving.

Picasso's Aubade, 1942

for Bruce McLeod

The musician is a flock
of triangles in which one

bird nests. The nude's a theory
of flesh: she can't possibly be

comfortable reclining like that,
but that's an abstraction I

can handle. It's the geometry
of the instrument that inflicts

pain, that brings the occupation
in. The text beside the painting

says: *The musician's posture suggests
his song of dawn has ended.* But look

again at the instrument—absent
of strings—dawn never begins.

Acorns

When his son—né
Rosenberg—began
to mow the lawn,

he cried out
for the acorns,
rescuing and planting

each in a coffee tin
beside the house.
122 saplings. This

was a small house,
the one to which
the boy and his brother

came home after the bomb-
shell of the execution.
Unable to kill anything

in his own garden, someone
said of Abel, who, seeing
Thomas Shipp and Abram Smith

lynched, couldn't look
away. Nearly any tree
can be a hanging tree,

nearly any garden—
tilled or pillaged—
can be one's own.

THREE

Lit

Everyone can't
be a lamplighter.

Someone must
be the lamp,

and someone
must, in bereaved

rooms sit,
unfathoming what

it is to be lit.

Silence

Not an absence
of blackbirds

singing, but
an abundance

of blackbirds
listening.

Closing

Give me one of those
glow-in-the-dark drinks.

I want to light
up my insides. Make

it a double: like you
and me, poured

out together, fluorescing.

Paid-Out

We say that when
there's nothing
left, because we still

have a tongue, hollowed
out, diminished as
it is, like the paid-

out vein of coal
that heats a stranger's
parlor far from here.

Virginal

That dress?
Look closer:

she sewed it
from a hundred

tattered flags
of surrender.

Slow Thinker

Audiences love the slow
        thinker, not the frozen
Rodin, but the flesh
        and bloodied one, the tragedian

in drag who gets kicked
        in the rear and hits
the pause button
        before bawling. Timing

is all in wowing
        the crowd: cry
when you see the kick
        coming, or the moment

the steel toe reaches
        you, and you lose them.
Abuse, to be humor,
        must come with a lag,

as if the pain were paid
        for on installment, as
if the pain came,
        not from the kick,

but from the slow
        boil of mulling it over.
Buster Keaton was a genius
        of slow thinking. He did

his own stunts, including
        a 17-year stint as a kid
getting kicked on stage
        by dear old dad. Back

then, they called the shtick
        Vaudeville, before Buster
and his mother called
        it quits, leaving pop to drop-

kick dead air, which got
        laughs for (at) Charlie Brown,
but not Pater Keaton. Buster, dead-
        panning, lived to make everyman

think he'd laughed at someone
        else, until, thinking a little
longer on the sadsack
        trying to build a house

inside a tornado, until
        the anesthesia of the heart
wore off, and everyman
        saw himself stumbling on.

Spec

Every body
gets built

this way.
Then you

wait to see
who moves in.

Still Life with Fast-Forward

Because I want to know
now: do the fruits

ripen? Do we?
Does someone fry

up the fish? Did it
die for no reason

other than us
gazing on its silver

scales forever? Is there
a forever? Are

we in it?

Stepping from Dream

Instead of the blue
wrapper of newspaper,

my hand grasps the hue
of hyacinth: in lieu of

cold and bottomless—
this azure raft.

What I Heard

She was talking about Akhmatova
and Mandelstam, how there

was only one egg, which she
gave him. But what I heard

was one *ache*: there was one
ache, and they shared it.

Station

If you'd asked,
as we sat

in a spring rain
of racing blossoms

at the station,
who do you love?

I'd have said:
I love the you

already on the train.
But that's a you

who didn't ask—I
loved her too.

My Raincoat Opens Doors for Me

It holds a door open above my head.
It's a door into the sky.

The raincoat enters before me,
as a man through revolving doors

at the Waldorf Astoria enters the past.
My raincoat can say *I love you*

more than technically possible
or wise in pine cone and French, in

dialects of peoples not yet invented.
It says this in the language of smashed

lamps and presto, the light reassembles.
There is another door, and another,

and there is only one me and one
raincoat and the peonies of doors that keep opening.

My Personal History

To guess it is to guess the number
of jelly beans in the basket and if
you guess right (or rightest), to win
the jelly beans, which look like
a rainbow cut up and packaged
for express delivery and guess what—
you don't like jelly beans or rainbows,
or you do, but you suffer
from color-blindness or diabetes and you
know that my personal history gets
boring around page eight, when I start
to explain the scars, which are
layered on top of all the other
scars you've met: some you won
in a contest, some were consolation
prizes. First prize is always the shoulder
to sigh on. When I was six and immortal,
Scott Blonder dared me to slide
down the water slide into the kidney-
shaped pool. If you do, he said,
Cocoa the poodle will bite you.
I did, Cocoa did, and Mrs. Blonder,
with orange merthiolate, painted a butterfly
on my left thigh. I can't show you
the butterfly, but I can show you its flight
pattern: away. That's how things find
their shape. There's a distance and we
get in line to funnel through it. You
can guess how many of us line up

at once, whether it's more or less
than the number of terracotta warriors
buried with their emperor. I saw
those figures exhibited in Brussels
last year, but they turned out to be
replicas, and who wants to pay
to see a replica of a replica? I've
got mirrors. I've got a personal history
with lint and layaway and oil fed
mistakenly into a basement
with a gas furnace. Things
blow up. Why am I telling you
this? Because dust is trying
to colonize my empire, because
I still have a few sleeves to fill
with tricks. Because I want you
to saw me in half in that French
construction worker's outfit you have
and then put me back together without
letting on that you've never done this
kind of thing before. I want this to be
something we laugh about before
it happens and afterwards, something
to amuse the deep snows long
after our coming and going.

FOUR

Overloaded

*for Edward J. Hogan, Yelena (Olena) Lisovich, and
Konstantin Lisovich*

It would have sufficed
to say our names, the name

of the lake, of those
we leave behind.

Yes, we took
too much: lunch, each

other, the boy's toy
bunny, the idea of traveling

the stretch we didn't know
Thoreau called *a wild-looking*

sheet of water, a wilderness he
crossed, barely, with Penobscot guide

in an *egg shell* of birch vessel.
By now you've guessed

how this ends: the over-
turning, the numbing

churning. That the canoe
was *overloaded*, as the news-

paper states, is true, but
to say so makes us seem

more culpable than human:
who among the living

pushes off without
surplus, without the abundant

conviction of paddling back?

Visiting the Cliffside Villa

People who live
alone have systems

for dishwashing, for the wringing
of hands. The dinner

bell or bell the cow
wears are not necessary.

Remember this if you visit.
Remember, when he stands, not

ungallantly, on the Brancusi
limestone chair, hanging

the mosquito net above
the bed. Remember, when

he clasps the lace mesh
to his chest as if it held

some slender bride. Try not
to forget how he harvests

the orange orchard single-
handed, how he lets

what he can't sell or eat,
under lock and key, in

the stone cellar, rot.

Little Circle as Placeholder

Andrea, I hear, as I'm running
near the sea and see John

running toward me, bulldog
in tow. I don't know, he says,

if you've met Zero, motioning
to the dog and the black spot

on his back, asking: What else
could I call him? Spot? I think, as

Zero trots off, as John and I run
after, calling the squat dog back

as he scrambles up dunes
through rosa rugosa.

You could call him Lorenzo
or Zac, call John Igor or me

Lavinia and still not scrub
the targets from our backs.

Fluoroscope

What drew us to shoe stores was the fluoroscope—
the not knowing, then knowing, which came

by placing your feet inside the wooden box.
Outside the box, your feet had secrets: where

they went, what held them together. Inside,
they revealed their insides, the scaffolding

of bone, the shape and stitching of new shoes
in which toes adjusted to show how they fit

or didn't. This was a fiction of course, a trick
of advertising that made us voyeurs, while exposing

everyone in proximity to the black
patent loafers and Mary Janes to crazy

doses of radiation. But the temptation to look
and exhibit comes in high doses too, this urge

to burn through flesh, so clerks & mothers & older sisters
stationed at portholes gazed at the horizon of light

and dark and no amount of commotion in perfume or ladies'
hats could compete with that X rating—the skeleton

come to life. I try to remember the price
of that joyride now, shifting on this front

porch from one nakedness to another,
begging entry to your lightning.

Exploratory

I know so little about you.
Do you keep llamas or migratory

birds against their will? How
little a person knows about

herself: I'm just learning, for
instance, how I'd ambush

starlings to impress you.
I'd press their wings inside

dictionaries or the DMS. Do you
have that manual beside your bed

of nails? I do, or did, until I met
the me your strangeness invents.

No entry describes obsessions
with creatures that come and go

seasonally, at nightfall, by instinct, by
virtue of wings, which, btw, are things

I don't have, or didn't until just now,
when I needed them to adjust the sun

above your timeshare/infrastructure. I
don't even know if this is the week you're

inside your body. I need more data:
do you respond to too much light

by fighting or flighting? What have
you learned from those birds you

do or don't tend? Enough
to fend this wrong night off?

Cliffside

At the Wicked Oyster, I
sit between Lou, who
builds seawalls, and Hugh,
who used to. Between
them is an encyclopedia
of hard engineering, of rubble
mounds and concrete armor.
We're sitting at the bar,
which is what people
without other people
do. Hugh drinks Coke,
Lou cozies his beer in foam.
They agree that static
features conflict with nature.
Once your neighbor builds,
you've got to build too,
because waves insist
on taking: it's a system
of accretion and loss.
They know that, their backs
and backhoes having
shifted mountains.
A finger in the dike,
Hugh says. Lou nods.
I'm trying to read
an article on grief. My
whiskey leaks into *trigger*,
into *time*. Today, cliffside,
I realized what fundamental

trade death makes: in lieu
of you, the memory of you.
Not fair, I'd say. Life
isn't, you said, or rather,
the memory of you
spoke, and wave upon
wave keeps repeating.

Beyond Consolation

After the seventh
death, Mary asks:
Burn or bury? Mary's
seven too, and doesn't
lose count. *How's
your faith?* a neighbor
asks. *Shaken,* she says,
*the way a snow globe
gets shaken.* People go
places and bring back
Palm Springs and Belize,
shrunken and flooded,
blizzard-ready. Mary's
taken to taking
to her room, shaking
Bali and Las Vegas,
every last exotica—
or call it balm—
contained, and by
design, whited out.

Propeller

To board the propeller plane, you
get to walk across the tarmac
like Cary Grant did or like you
did in your own innocent past.
By you, of course, I mean me, meaning
to imply a kind of universal you-
ness and me-ness, a linkage suggesting
we're together on this tarmac, eyeing
the propeller suspiciously because
the thing that can take you
into the future can take
your head off too. In this
instance it doesn't, and I take
my seat in 7D, beside a man
named Bob who can taste my
faithlessness, explaining how
he racks up frequent flyer miles
for Jesus and how some of his best
friends are Jewish accordion players.
I tell him that some of my best
pick-up lines for women come
from the Bible. *I wonder*, he asks:
New or Old Testament?
I show him scribbling that may
fester into admissions
of love or smaller manifestos. Some
are in French: *Je t'aime quand même.*
He asks me to translate. *I love you
anyway*, I say. He blushes because

no one, except Jesus, has ever
said that to him. I think I'd like to be
one of his sheep, to be sheared
and grass-fed, to lose my way
so he can find me. Up in the air, where
we're from is stripped from us.
I tell him another Bob—a minor
god, but major Bob—Bob Hicok—
is coming to fetch me in Roanoke.
That Bob likes his autumn
shaken and stirred, he likes it
with a side of blizzard, with dollops
of dirt and confetti. He eats it
with a pitch fork and a tuning fork,
wearing SuperBob boots and cape,
telling the vultures that get
too close to the joy mobile he
is to take a hike. Like non-
Bobs, he's aged: time's devoured
the chocolate pudding that was
his pompadour, leaving an unguarded
pate a sea bird strayed far inland
mistakes for a place to break the mussel
hauled all this way—which is
to say I'm aware of feasting
and famine, of the breakage
both entail. I believe that faith
may be a question of giving
oneself to a series of men

named Bob, men who look
upon turbulence as a kind
of amusement ride, men who
don't want to convert me so
much as share the beauty
that spills out from them, including
the secret handshake the Bobs
of the world mean to make
unsecret, as Bob the pastor hands me over
to Bob the poet, as the vultures back off
across the Clinch River, momentarily,
and the green of western Virginia,
like an endless landing strip, unspools.

Another Q & A

We like symmetry
in faces, a kind of echo-
location that says two
halves—miraculous!—have found
each other. I found the car
after a long time searching
the parking lot. I couldn't find
the me who'd parked it.
I gave you something
broken so you wouldn't
worry about it breaking.
We get an extra hour
of light and it feels
like the extra shoe
the one-legged man gets.
What do we do
with our hands?
Not being in love
is a lot like soccer—lots
of stumbling and head-butting.
I like the idea of the Q&A,
which suggests a balance
sheet of call and response,
but too often the questions
are just lonely people
standing at the microphone
saying, I'm lonely, and the wise
woman at the lectern nodding.

Mayflower Heights

The house on the hill existed
before the hill. We built
the hill for a better view

of ourselves, Hopperesque,
from the flats. Beneath the house
(built on stilts) is a yellow bicycle,

a Schwinn, circa 1960, capable
of going up and downhill, which is
to say into the past and future.

The bike's locked to a beam.
It's a combination lock.
How long has it been?

If I try to recall, across all these
seasons, the series of numbers
needed to release that lock,

I'll forget the other numbers
I'm keeping. Numbers are like
sheep, or we think that because

we want to be shepherds.
5-19-5. There, you have it: the yellow
sun of the bicycle, the twenty-year-

old me pedaling beside the sea,
the salt-bright night, the hill, the winding
fire road, by bittersweet, overtaken.

Amsterdam, Hotel Silton

Three missed trains
before we got there.
Missing each other
at the bus stop,
at the station.
Hash under glass.
A chicken—if not
in every pot—in
ours, in the dining
room, by the requisite
fire, the red wine
redder and redder.
When at last
we went upstairs,
all the doors
on all the floors
were open—as
if nothing could
be forbidden.
It was. I
forgive you.

Naming the Animals

Rover, Lucky, Charles.
Like movie stars, the dogs
and cats get one name.
The children try naming
the cows and pigs.
Best not to, we say,
not explaining the logic
of attachment and slaughter.
In Warsaw, we're on a first-
name basis with the dead,
the memorial unable
to contain the magnitude
of erasure, so what we've
got is the 400 names
most commonly given
and taken: Hanna, Alter,
Malech. It's 1988. I'm
standing inside the monument
made to represent an open
train car. The cars that took
Oskar and Eta and Abel
from the Umschlagplatz
opened their doors
to Treblinka. It's winter.
I'm writing the names
in a notebook I'll lose
somewhere over the Atlantic.
But the names aren't lost.
Eliahu, Rita, Celina.

It's taken me 25 years
to know what to do:
say them. Symcha
and Reuben and impish
Pinkas, just beginning
to name his animals.

Camera Obscura

It's the movie where everything
happens without you: your wife
on the sidewalk, wondering what
she's forgotten, your son trying
to retrieve a postcard dropped
in the box, a dog slipping
its leash, your daughter
not looking both ways, a red
flag flapping. It all happens
as you sit in a darkened room
formerly used for storage. You
are a darkened room formerly
used for many purposes. It happens
upside down and backwards, in
Technicolor, in full sun, and seems
to be happening in the past,
so you can't alter or enter
the chain of events. Wittgenstein
said a body couldn't experience
itself falling through space,
but you feel pain in the pricked
room as Main Street parades past,
as if projected onto a train slowly
leaving the station. Such a flood
of melancholy, of nostalgia
for what never was or will be.
Surely the Germans have a word

for that, surely someone in another
dark room is composing a symphony
on the topic. It's a requiem, atonal.
Your wife, glancing up, appears to hear it.

Isn't True Love Wonderful?

Ecobutch from Cornish just made me her favorite,
which is more than I can say of Kitchenslut100
or 101. Ecoslut might be the one
for me, and because of the wonders
of wondering, I can click
on pixels of my affection all
night and see their private
peccadilloes rise beneath my touch.
One likes fisting, another vanilla
ice cream licked from her hair.
Where do people come
from, where do they get
fetishes for tomboys in stilettos?
I don't know what I like until I've seen it
on a pillow 300 days in a row. It's ok
to wash the pillowcase as long as it spins
in counterintuitive ways—we all have
idiosyncrasies, if not mates. My
notmates are many, and we share
so much: birth month, love for loose-
fitting modifiers, close-ups long
on soft focus. Most employ
the selfie, which shouts how
alone they are, unless you count
vitamin supplements and hair gels
on bathroom counters. Context
matters, and in a finite you-
and-me verse, I need to hurry
and admit I love you and how

does anyone rappel out
of herself into another without grave
risks? You have a habit of tilting
your brain back, with a question.
You have a body with windows
and doors and once you left
the lights on in there, the way
people in Amsterdam in tall, slender
houses on sleepy canals will, without
draperies, a kind of invitation, a way
of saying I have nothing
to hide. I appreciate now how
you take the long way from A
to A, how you believe Z or hyacinths
or maps to crumbled places may
figure into it. I'm trying to articulate
my lack of attraction to people
trying to do things. Would you like
to love me without trying? That's
an abstract proposition that ought
to come with an airline ticket
and an overhead compartment.
I want to go away with you so we
can come home together, so we can stand
at passport control and have the man
in the glass booth glance from our papers
to the clock on the wall, back to us, and ask,
as the maître d' once did to my first sweetheart
and me at The Lark Supper Club

outside of Iowa City in 1985: *Isn't*
true love wonderful? It is, and after
the man waves us on toward the carousel,
after we claim our suitcases and the beagle
named Rex trained to sniff out
heroin and pears and illicit French
cheeses makes a beeline
for me, unbidden, I'll unzip
myself, letting all my
light, for anyone in this
dark world to trip over.

* 1- Jones move up?
* 2- USC dvs.— Curtube?
  3- donations?
  4- 2500 - 3500 Jane C?
  5- Jane Head
  6- Alice O.
  7- Paris Review
    _ Canadian! - 2 poems
  8 Archie Cohen
  9 - M Rhodes?
  * - Aimee — no Dorothy poem
  * - Eric - Walter
  * - Any book cover
  * -

Acknowledgements

I am grateful to the editors of these journals, in which the following poems appeared, sometimes in slightly different incarnations.

Alaska Quarterly Review: "What I Heard"; *American Poetry Review:* "Isn't True Love Wonderful?"; *Barn Owl Review:* "State of the Nation"; *Beloit Poetry Journal:* "Doing the Loop," "Poison Hotline"; *Berfrois:* "Porch Swing, Summer in a Glass"; *Construction:* "Silence," "Visiting the Cliffside Villa"; *The Cincinnati Review:* "Bedside"; *Diode:* "Branch Water," Abandoned House," "Q&A," "String Theory," "Door-to-Door," "Cliffside," "Picasso's Aubade, 1942," "In Response To," "Acorns," "Or Pinocchio (When Inside the Whale)," "Propeller"; *Lost Wknd:* "The Fall of Lawless Bodies"; *Ibbetson Press:* "Fluoroscope"; *The New Yorker:* "Easter on the Rio Grande," "Lit"; *Orion:* "Where the Sugar Dollars"; *Ploughshares:* "Task Lighting"; *Plume:* "My Personal History," "My Raincoat Opens Doors for Me," "Slow Thinker"; *Poetry Daily:* "Doing the Loop"; *Provincetown Arts:* "Camera Obscura," "Station"; *Salamander:* "Puzzle," "Still Life with Fast Forward," "Outage," "Tornado," "Still Life"; *Salmon Poetry 35th Anniversary Anthology:* "Amsterdam, Hotel Silton"; *Terminus:* "Exploratory," "Anyone into Anything"; *Terrain:* "Overloaded," "Mayflower Heights"; *The Threepenny Review:* "Naming the Animals"; *Upstreet:* "Little Circle as Placeholder"; and *Washington Square Review:* "Flow Chart," "Vocation".

Lamplighters: Francesca Bewer, Gail Mazur, Gail Caldwell, Barbara and Andrew Senchak, Maja, Fay, Alma, Edith and Dominic Green, Amy Anderson, Danielle Jones-Pruett, Rebecca Morgan Frank, Giavanna Munafo, and my family. Thanks to Martha Rhodes and the folks at Four Way, and all hats off to The MacDowell Colony. And Naomi Wallace, you still rock.

Andrea Cohen's poems and stories have appeared in *The Atlantic Monthly, Glimmertrain, The Hudson Review, The New Republic, The New Yorker, Poetry, The Threepenny Review,* and elsewhere. Her earlier poetry collections include *The Cartographer's Vacation, Long Division, Kentucky Derby,* and *Furs Not Mine.* She directs the Blacksmith House Poetry Series in Cambridge, MA and the Writers House at Merrimack College.

Publication of this book was made possible by grants and donations. We are also grateful to those individuals who participated in our 2016 Build a Book Program. They are:

Anonymous (8), Evan Archer, Sally Ball, Jan Bender-Zanoni, Zeke Berman, Kristina Bicher, Carol Blum, Lee Briccetti, Deirdre Brill, Anthony Cappo, Carla & Steven Carlson, Maxwell Dana, Machi Davis, Monica Ferrell, Martha Webster & Robert Fuentes, Dorothy Goldman, Lauri Grossman, Steven Haas, Mary Heilner, Henry Israeli, Christopher Kempf, David Lee, Jen Levitt, Howard Levy, Owen Lewis, Paul Lisicky, Katie Longofono, Cynthia Lowen, Louise Mathias, Nathan McClain, Gregory McDonald, Britt Melewski, Kamilah Moon, Carolyn Murdoch, Tracey Orick, Zachary Pace, Gregory Pardlo, Allyson Paty, Marcia & Chris Pelletiere, Eileen Pollack, Barbara Preminger, Kevin Prufer, Peter & Jill Schireson, Roni & Richard Schotter, Soraya Shalforoosh, Peggy Shinner, James Snyder & Krista Fragos, Megan Staffel, Marjorie & Lew Tesser, Susan Walton, Calvin Wei, Abigail Wender, Allison Benis White, and Monica Youn.